MY
UGLY &
OTHER
LOVE
SNARLS

HELL PRESS
UNIVERSITY OF HELL PRESS

MY UGLY & OTHER LOVE SNARLS

Wryly T. McCutchen

HELL PRESS
UNIVERSITY OF HELL PRESS

This book published by University of Hell Press.
www.universityofhellpress.com

© 2017 Wryly T. McCutchen

Cover and Interior Design by Olivia Croom
http://bit.ly/oliviacroom

All rights reserved. No part of this book may be
reproduced or transmitted in any form or by
any means, electronic or mechanical, including
photocopying, recording or by any information
storage and retrieval system, without written
permission from the publisher, except for the
inclusion of brief quotations in a review.

Published in the United States of America.
ISBN 978-1-938753-24-4

Contents

Dedication: Putting Gender in Context

Dedication:
Putting Gender in Context

Since writing most of the work that follows, I've begun a path of transition away from womanhood. My name is different, my body is going through changes, and the language I use has shifted considerably. This may sound familiar to some but my transgender story isn't stereotypical. I never felt trapped by my body, just bigger; like everyone I know, who I am is so much more than just my body. I have few regrets and little disconnect from the person I used to be. I am grateful for the experiences I had when I was a girl. I could not be who I am today without them. These poems would not have been possible any other way.

This book is for a lot of people: my partner Strand, my parents, my brother Allen, and my sisters Ariel and Kerry. This book is also for everyone who has ever toiled and rejoiced their way through the blistering deliciousness of womanhood. It's a celebration and a breakup letter; a milepost at the end of a lengthy journey with women who welcomed me, cherished me, and molded me. In fleeting moments, I still mourn the lost lusciousness of being your sister. But this is the end of us. My wheels are meant for other roads now. Thank you. My time within your midst left me with a beautiful ache, one that characterizes both my writing and the way I move along on this earth.

JP   10·5·18

It's been years since I've
written with a gel pen.
Thank you always, for your
juicy thoughts & suggestions
I love our artistic kinship.
And I rejoice in the depth &
spice of our connection.
You are truly fascinating,
tender & true. ♡

Recipe Meditation

Tonight the dishwasher will go wild,
rumbling with the ambition of too-large bowls.
Using too many ingredients is my favorite kind of sin
chopped audacity makes each turn of the pot
       precarious
with peas
carrots
mushrooms
potatoes
& a generous handful of thyme.

Cut them all into knuckle-sized hunks,
angle spatula towards alchemy.
Thick & herbed
let the meal come to life
slowly
as the oven arches its back
& the biscuits ache to be kneaded.

Happy List

My tongue can be a whistle
Pickle juice gulped straight from cool twist of a jar's
        mouth
The sound of smooth rocks talking as the ocean pulls
        back
Just letting cool water run between my thumb &
        forefinger
The way my breath calms gradually after climbing a
        hill
The empty in my lungs after I shout
The heft of machines whose jobs are imperceptibly
        large
Being any part of a sandwich hug
but especially the middle
Sunlight between thighs
Anything that even reminds me of a bicycle
Pistons pumping
Close-cropped white beards
Playing horseshoes with my father
Remembering that words are just containers waiting
        to be filled
Boots that fit snug
Red & blue tattoos that remind me that we all have
Veins &
Capillaries draining &
Arteries endlessly rushing onward

My Butch

My butch is budding.
At night my butch
crawls out & curls
up in my bra to suck
out the day's yellow longing sweat.

My butch loves meat
& would nail your body
hot & skinfull to the nearest wall
if you bought her a cheeseburger.

My butch guffaws proudly at farts.

My butch can be both tender & creatively
rough. My butch will ignite
sweat between your breasts.
Her eyes will dance at changes in your breath.
My butch has a firm grasp on your shoulder.
She's not afraid to clutch ankles
or use hipbones as a tuning fork.

My butch is budding
large & proud down to every follicle
my butch smiles knowingly
when pedestrians notice

her fuzzy undercarriage.
My butch is irritated by underwear
that is anything less than comfortable.

My butch tells me that my cock
looks better
with a little bit of belly hanging over.
All push back &
crafty syllogisms, my butch
makes love like retaliation.

My butch always keeps lubricant handy
in case the gears get thirsty.
My butch tells me not to downshift
that the pain my ass will
ache when morning
comes is worth the climb.
And that my legs
deserve to be bigger.

My butch tells me
that being a happy mussel
is more important than suffering pearls.
And then she laughs like emptied abalone clacking.

My butch tells me
sweat is just evidence
of love & dignity.

My butch loves
the dirt.
My butch thinks poppies
about to burst look
just like nipples, throbbing fuzzily in the breeze.

My butch is budding.

Skin from Skin

There is always
distinction between lip & salt
granular packing heavy
shined pearl in the

mouth is just a cut
that grew its ambitions
white & stinging into
something or other.

The ocean of language is constant
reincarnation. Clash
symbols tighten the air. The
mollusks calibrate their tongues

burrowed deep
making out
words harsh the sound
slaps wet against lip.

The other is a rib echo
skin from skin
your gender against my gender
conventions jumble

where barnacles gather
with frail fingers
hungry for cleanse
& gargle of salt.

To My Red Rusthoney

I missed you all those months you hung in the dark of my parents' shed. I'm writing to tell you: you are so much more than a forgotten Frisbee or broken roller skates.

I want you to know that everybody compliments your saddle. You've got me habitually tucking laces in. The day won't even start without a cuffed pant leg.

Yesterday, I gave you hustle and we whistled through all the lights in south SoDo. When we whizzed over the pavement gaping open its steel-throated railroad tracks, I could hear the voice of your spokes buzzing. Your mousy calls out, lets me know where to apply the appropriate fluids. I'll need to grease you soon.

I know the rain might get you down, but I am here for you, my lovely. Your rust spots are just freckles. I love your vermilion splotches. I love you when your churning parts fall through. I love you even when my slow hands can't fix everything. I love you fenderless, rain and rubble dusting my chin without apology. When you spin grit into my mouth, I remember that the street is still beneath me.

Perched precarious I push your balance down and down. You return motions tenfold like the hollow magic of moon gravity. Built up lactic acid releases tensions combustible. My calves are starting to resemble rockets and that nook between my ass and hip (you know the place), well, that place is aching in the shape of our voyages.

I promise I'll make some time to love you this week. I'll push, you carry.

You dizzy me with spinning spinning spinning. Wet with the journey of us, my darling red rusthoney, I dream of you asleep in the basement. Not lying down, but tilted. Your front wheel cocked and whispering, "Ride, ride, ride."

Elle

I gobble down her bookshelf
as tender as any sex
stick fingers through pages.

I have this vision,
we go to a queer dreamland.
Breasted hijinks ensue.

I could tell that's where she most liked being touched.
How lung
released from lips as I gripped
too much &
weak knees returned,

eyelids boiled skyward
heart bent red gush fingers up voicebox
I might give out just thinking about

when leaned against kitchen table
I readied shivers
& buckled under.

Red table that
met both our hips exactly
where we split the echoes of her refrigerator,

our legs go
all the way up.

When she buckled
I lifted, moved fast
& strong like alligator.
I know exactly how much I can hold.

A small constellation of freckles
on legs shimmered sharp
pushing up skirt
olive tights with stirrup keeping steady

our rhythm simmered with fist
in hair, contact tugging
neckline. Happily,
I noticed how
we noticed each
other.

This spring

the daylight is a series of chasers.
As my skin gathers up its bright red hangover
the sun is drowning like a grapefruit,
& the vodka is coming,
certain as the moon,
the robust bottles,
they are coming.

The wine will turn you
into freckles brown
patches flaking.
Tonight's sheets will be
a blizzard of sun-drunk skin.

Our burns cook off in the night,
like the lilac vodka we soaked our French toast in.
The Calendar's widening its eyes.
The horizon's got infinity on its breath.
We duck that florid purpling afterglow,
begin fucking in the blossomed yawn of a cherry tree.

Bodies' colors tilted by
sunshine now liver-crimson,
you cracked so beautifully
when I poured my freckles over you.

Letter to a Young Coyote

Don't stop. Your deep fish-filled lungs tug at my river's underbelly. Your words are a brush fire kept in a safety deposit box. Your words are a rattlesnake's skin left to crisp along Highway 2.

Remember that Ellensburg cop? We'd been speeding and he tried to impress us. Rolled up his sleeves and said, "You know, this is the most dangerous stretch of road in all of Washington?" As hard as we laughed at his overblown badge shine, I realize he's right.

This road is not safe. This highway of sound uncontrollably hooking together is so dangerous my teeth begin chattering away like 10,000 typewriters. There are coyotes waiting in the wings. I'll need you to keep an eye out for switchbacks and the thick-edged fists of basalt.

This road, sunk between impending architecture and a hard unforgiving sun, bakes history into skin.

Under all this I am waiting for my paycheck to waste away. I am here to watch its meaning whittled down to a stub. I am here anyway.

I am here for your words. Hot, strong, and dangerous words. Words that wedge me deeper between burnt rocks and howling hard places. I am here for skidded asphalt syllables. I am here for the words that will never be comfortable in the mouth of the holster. I am here to get loaded with the words that put bullet holes in my paradigms.

I want you with me all the way because your words are dangerous and unbankable and your words have got coyotes in their throats. Your words are a revolution running down your lips.

And we passed the last ATM days ago.

This highway is dangerous, but honey I am here for all its swerves and potholes. Got your pen marks scratched inside my ribcage. The back seat stocked deep with heavy-measured breaths. We are moving forward with empty pockets and broken ballpoints. We are driving open our mouths—our bodies together flex into the journey position.

Eventually the hungry pocket of horizon gobbles down ferocious sun. This road is my religion, my ritual exchange. I trust your arrival is coming. Because your words have got incredible currency.

When you asked about the gift of violence

other poets spoke first.

I could name at least ten
ideas I would have found intolerable
or incomprehensible and frightening,
except as they came
after dreams
and poems...[1] like the impatient thump
which unexpectedly restores
the picture to the television set, or
the electric shock which sets the fibrillating
heart back to its proper rhythm.[2]

Poetry breaks through. Poetry does
more than those dime store narratives.
Poetry finds exactly
where you are most inflexible, then
it'll ask you to bend.

With cat tongue poetry licks
in, abrasive on your tender, pumps
your lungs into believing they're gravity's
victims. It's all poetry's fault.

---

1 Audre Lorde, *Poetry Is Not a Luxury.* 1984.
2 Seamus Heaney, *Crediting Poetry.* 1995.

Poetry knows there is damage to be done.
That the fall is necessary.
That our kneecaps require better colors for selling.

Poetry, the perfect product, gives you
exactly what you want before you want it
because poetry is the process by which your
            wanting is shifted.

Poetry opens your capacity for healing
cuts your whole body
into a mouth, hungry for
the risk & rupture.

There is a crack, a crack in everything
That's how the light gets in.[1]

Poetry is the opposite
of a parachute; giving in
to skinned knee, broken femur,
& hot white insides pouring out.

The wound is the place where the Light enters you.

---

1   Leonard Cohen, *Anthem*. 1992.

Smokeless Fires

We met in the suicide season
fresh of resolutions
festering bellyside.
Cigarette ghosts still clung
to your frantic
fingers & their knitting
multicolor rectangles longing for the caress of neck
you reduced desire knot after knot.

Hands cracked like mine
like they understood the difficulty of loosening.

I came to you
holes acid-burned
in stomach, voice soured from too long
in the cellar.
I came to you a hibernation
sunrise; acid pink disaster tearing up horizon
from there the mercury only got heavier.

We met in the suicide season.

I came to you pretenses flimsy
& we wrestled our devils out among the Jack Frosts
found words to reconcile by

found sounds to strike our
smokeless fires alive.

A Brand New Box of Matches

She's got hornets
in her throat & lizards in her
feet. Face smiles guttural
howl of a churchyard motorcycle.
You can tell it's winter by the thick
of her exhaust pumping.

She is cowboy boots two sizes too small,
blistered histories that tried so
hard to Cinderella
she stepped on her
sisters. Kissed the wrong fellow
& covered the hiss of her
snakish mistake in the yellow
mouth of a match strike.

Deflowering

In the corner of the room a pink
model, translucent
arrangement of plastic
reproduction
flowers clean, mute, & smooth.

Disrobing, I shimmy out
of its view & naked
from waist down I lay awkward,
crumple of paper coverings.

"Just breathe deeply here."
I chuckle, "Ouch," &
Tough Guy shudder, toes twinging.

They tell me,
"It's okay
   to say ouch."

I small talk pain,
"Did you know that tulips
   were Europe's very first
   commodity bubble?"

Lips parted, the anecdote's
dark pollen is working.

Speculum pressures
prehensile pocket
& disinfect cervix
with thin nimble

tools. "You're doing really
good. Almost
done.

The pain should subside
in about 24 hours."

At the counter, I flash
my State Services card
& slide under plastic partition
a guilty five-dollar bill.

Pockets now too empty for a cab,
I stumble doped
as over-the-counter
meds can get. The air so thick
with pollen, I choke home weeping.

This morning

I first pulled off my flannel pajama top. Second, shuffled jeans over thigh in a false start, never popping them over frowning buttocks and pimpled hip. I got too tired. Or maybe I tripped while trying to sip coffee and pull up my pants. Third, I shivered the black denim back into a crumple at the foot of the bed. Fourth, I picked up and inserted myself into the still warm armholes of my flannel pajama top. Fifth, I buttoned the buttons askew.

Back in bed I drank the remaining coffee so slowly the last two sips were as cold as zippers in winter.

Carry On

Tendered finger
pads thirst, hungry through
downpour, for a quench that sticks

for a quench that is more than just a fix.

I tighten my spokes to compromise,
push forward my broken,
my lopsided,
my good enough to carry on
parts.

If I prayed, this would
be what I prayed about.

Press palms & tendered lifelines together.
Hold my threadbare,
my chicken-wire emergency
fixes.

Carry me through the callous of adventure
or at least let the
crack of catastrophe happen
swiftly, let the gift of violence
befall me while riding tender
concrete.

My Ugly

I move into the mirror. I
accept everything
to be opposite. Unsurprised
by reversals. I expect
my forehead below my hipbones
reach past my bangs to touch thigh.

I'm not thinking about dancing.
I thin myself still, watch the way
my patterns refuse to line
up. I tug, shift, purse,
grimace & bear teeth
then swift run tongue pink over
their crooked. With my reversal's
expectations quenched, the mirror me
has got the eyes of
everyone I've ever met. I told them
all proudly
that I've learned to love my crooked smile,

but really I've only taught it to strut
dressed it up in a quaint progression,
smoothed over its toothy yellow jutting
so it seems a quirk I've always meant.

My reflection approaches
from the muted shut of elevator door,
shows up expectant in shop windows.
Compulsed to, as quick as possible,
I remake & reframe & redress.
I feel need for change tugging.

Beauty comes over me quick
I am not thinking
my mouth moves like tic
every time I ritual my smile:
Tongue over teeth slips
chin dips
eye sharpen,
& grasp desperate to beauty's breast.

In the mirror I can't be ugly.
I am only potential.
I am work to be done.

I mutilate my ugly
pimple by pimple
I break my skin
each time, refuse my ugly.

if there's a mirror in sight my ugly can feel
beauty & its gears wrenching
into artifice.

My ugly always keeps a bag
packed. My ugly's hands are always ready
for survival. My ugly is used to the refusals.
My ugly forgets the salt
of acceptance.
Ugly is what tore you open
a little, ugly is what tears open
the language of opposites
inspires the raw
larynx into flutterings of dissent & magnificence.

I don't think we can reclaim beauty.
Beauty is a fever in need
of constant breaking.
Beauty was forged
in the language of opposites,
in a window's empty. Beauty wants you
to believe in nothing else but motion.

Forget how to be. Beauty always needs
more. Addicted to forward, hooked on
concepts of contrast. Beauty wants you
to forget stillness.

In the high gloss & hot rush of media
beauty asks you to
believe that the ugly exists only
to affirm her heat.

But if, when ugly does
break this beauty fever

I can become so magnificently ugly.

Ugly is a cold compress,
it is thick,
it is dirty,
it has mud under its fingernails.
Soaked in the foul of nourishing salts
this ugly knows healing secrets.

Beauty loves to lie.
Beauty fever will wrap fingers
around the ugly's budding,
try to make it hot.
Beauty will steal, cut, & press
ugly parts into service, into shine.

But no.
My ugly,
my crooked teeth,
my thick wrists & puffy cheeks
my too-small head & pockmarked bottom
my inner thigh jungle
my cracked beauty fever is not a quirk.

My ugly is not catharsis.
My ugly, under all the submission it's been beaten into,
has got bigger plans.

In the slow quiet between
beauty's chronic doing,
my ugly & I soft lock gaze.
She winks slow, eyes crusted
thick with the wisdom
that the beauty beast is still coming.

My ugly says calmly,
"Carry with you these words:
Next time at the mirror
when the pressed thin request
nudges your thick into profile,
when the crooked gapping of tooth
threatens to make beauty with your tongue,
open your mouth
wider just look.
Take in the thick.
Take in the yellowing crooked.
Open & tell your tongue
we are no longer feeding this
beauty fever."

Left Hand Poem

Shift switch
working on
like sliding slip-jaw
gnawing down what's between
teeth.

There's restrictions on speed.
Our wrist distance doesn't fluctuate.
Push grip
under the habit.

This is the same ritual.
Flipped its risk,
skims inches above atrophy.

The waiting muscle paces
in parallel
longs its eyes; its transmission
hungry to corrupt.

Resist.

Trust your fingers.
Trust your feet.
Their bones know slowness

is not nothing.
They know to keep

going.

Others Are Resting

I used to sleep.
I am used
to sleep. Sleek use peels
away. I'll sleep
when I'm dead. I will sleep
when I am used to the soft peel of death.

There is no longer any
sense in resting. Work on
death while others are resting.
Find fallow only at your final
exhaustion. The dénouement
of your use
must be put off indefinitely.
Sleep plunges & slowly
peels off the root of your use.

I am working on not sleeping.
I am working on death.
I am working the rest away.
I used to sleep

but in these days of use
my alarm
clock is always ringing.

"Too bad you'll never make a living at it."

At nine(teen)
my ambition had rose petals stuffed
in her mouth & lace wrapped
around her ankles. We muffled her
with romantic jingles about a more sensible degree,
told her she could really come
out when we'd saved enough to make it to Paris,
then we hid her body in a trunk.

And now it's all crashing down
with the smell of decomposing romance.
Turns out there's no money there
in the murder or the hiding.

I open her chest & harvest her upturned corners
whenever a customer needs to see more than
just my teeth.
We're afraid the managers might notice her there,
because she started eating kicked-away nickels
the register missed.

Behind the counter
her feathers are fluxing & cruxing,
but we stuck her hands in the dishwater,
made her dance in the broom closet

stuffed her feelers into a hairnet.

She gets quieter as
the rent check clears up
her understanding of our shared financial empty.

Still, she remembers how to speak French
& readies my hands for the fast
of intuitive dancing.

Once again we stifle her
frenzied speed, anchors stillness
beneath the fingernails. Open
palmed I invite the widening
empty of pleats & pockets & purses.

Stilled, all her dreams steep like tea.
Haggard & gray she waits
her alphabet hammers are hungry to bruise.

Babydoll & Spatula

Mama bear's bed
is always too soft.

As Goldilocks' body yields to puberty
her bed will grow softer too,
because a woman's bed is
bruised into being
soft
enough
to welcome in
the whole of humanity's
guilt in need of healing.

The same motion
that fills her golden bosom
with babydoll & spatula
leaves her brother's arms
empty for functions of destruction
& braced for scars
to be wept over in private.

Goldilocks, shoulders now
wet with tears entitled & uninvited,
learns to keep her dried-up eyes
always open to
the burden of absolute nurture.

Her muscles ache from that
old habit of reflexively bearing
witness.

Her vagina will provide a sturdy basement
for a temple of the world's discontent.
And she'll learn
a woman's compassion is at everyone's disposal.

One day, Goldilocks will learn to
stop exploring,
& down her throat will be
forced the cold porridge of concern

with a simple ubiquitous script:
when you see her toddling legs,
tell her first how pretty she looks.
Say nothing else,
then scoop her up
with forearms hot.

Tell her, "Smile,"
while she cries.

Call her, "Bitch," because,
"You'll catch more flies with honey, Honey."

Congratulate her coy susceptibility.
Always call on her
when you feel
need pushing
from beneath
your skin.

Tie her coming-of-age into an apron
of dainty acquiesces,
ready her hands for the wooden spoon
& the porridge
always too cold.

Primer for the Docent of the Doubled Atrium/Ventricle Mechanism

I.
In the museum of the body
the heart is considered the most staggering of
        biomechanical marvels:
The Mona Lisa of our soft insular world,
because it is & can so often
be stolen.

II.
As some of you may know
from visits to dimmer
less sacred bodies,
a museum without its centerpiece leeches ennui
into its very floorboards.
Longing hangs heavy in the doorways.
A structure without a hearty pump is merely a
        deathbed nicely adorned.

III.
In infancy, the heart develops at breakneck speed.
Its complexity coils quickly,
week
after week
after week

after week
& then punches a smallish
heart-shaped hole on the ultrasound.
It begins to mimic beats instantly.
And when fully grown
can recognize & match the rhythms
of its kin from several fathoms apart.

IV.
The inspiring allure
hearts so easily harbor
has little to do with the technique & design of the
        heart itself.
The heart's allure is most reliably conjured up
by the frequency with which it has been stolen away
to collect adventure & bruises at the hands of
        gentle highwaymen.
Everyone loves a heart with a bit of a renegade past.

V.
Although not the oldest piece in our collection
    (i) that would be the digestive tract
which opened first as a tunnel of folded-over flesh
        & yolk
& then became the basement & foundation
home to cave paintings & sculptures burbling in
        porous stone & prehistory,
nor is the heart the softest part

(ii) that would be the liver.
Cynics love the liver,
& idolize its dingy dance into martyrdom.
Inscribed below the liver exhibit (in both Russian &
       English) are the words:
"I am a sick man. I am a spiteful man."
Contrary to popular belief the heart is not the most
       sensitive part of the body either,
   (iii) that would be the tissue on genitals & lips.
While not above a hearty tingle or two,
an organ as central & magnanimous as the heart
knows not to hoard sensational currents
& releases to the lips
a rush of hot-blood encouragement.

VI.
While it isn't the most sensitive,
the heart is perhaps the organ most often damaged,
the piece of the machine
susceptible to the widest array of possible pains inflicted.

VII.
It is important to note that because of the high sensitivity
the heart has developed
an endurance for lengthy & catastrophic discomfort,
as well as an incredible resilience seen nowhere else
       in the body.

VIII.

Weighing in at less than a pound,
it has strength enough to move masses
up to 3,000 times its own weight.
The four chambers of its miraculous architecture
were built with equal parts openness & solid musculature
& then duplicated
ventricle for ventricle
atrium for atrium.
specifically designed to support itself
when one of its four rooms have been
ravaged,
poisoned,
or
occupied by dangerous intents.
A heart with four intentions will
never fold or break,
it can only be bruised.[1]

---

1   Seeded from Buddy Wakefield's poem *We Were Emergencies*. "...hearts don't break,/y'all,/
they bruise & get better."

Hate is born in the mouth

of a hornet, whose nest has
been knocked from heaven.

Reminder

I know you want to reconcile. You always want to reconcile and that is one of most beautiful things about you ... but the soaking, remember you are soaking. You don't have to stop or hurry into reconciliation.

When you draw from your watershed to brine puffy sorrows you should also draw a border. Draw a circle of woe—protect your process from easy solutions and the ready warmth of loved ones.

Be greedy with your grief.

No one will think less of you. They might miss you, but, discomfort isn't always an invitation to cultivate, and sometimes sadness is just your feelings asking to lie fallow for a while.

This time keep your catastrophe inside the container of you. Don't let the possibility of another knocking convince you that you are alone. You've got yourself. Stay there. Do the work.

Wash away the myths lodged in your optic nerve and stuck echoing in the slurry of ear bones. Don't let their nervous knocking for a second interrupt your journey toward the sound of "enough." You are enough.

You aren't bad and you don't need anybody to fix or validate you. You don't need a sounding board or a rational answer; that is not where you are going right now. You'll get there if you choose. But right now you're working towards enough. Your muscle memory will echo confidence until you get there. You will get there.

You are already enough, just take this moment and let your feelings catch up.

In There

I can't stop remembering the peek
of nut brown, out
from under eyelashes cutting
sharp behind the comfort
of folded arm. You
blush covert so that only
I can notice. First I ask then

scoot, tuck in. I soft
contact my side against yours, I can
tell, today, more than most days
you are in there,

a bit bristled but in there.
Happy to feel my ribcage
breathing into your breath.

I can't stop remembering
how I knew this was intimate,
even more so than the last time
we kissed & we are just
touching

exchanging words about labor & use
& what it means to be human

when there are things to be
done.

We kiss once, closed
mouth only, before I leave
you & I think furtively
of dragging you into embrace of
alleyway, where no one would see
how I stick my fingers in your gender.

Sriracha

I know I am supposed to
go. My fingers turn key & exhaust
coughs out rasping Rooster backfire.
The engine is thin,
fueled by too many favors
whose trajectories pull
tender the tension of us.

The bathwater morning
fills up my ears. I am only
gulps now
as the engine slowly turns
over. There are roses
in the basement & a saffron song
chiseled up my sternum.
She's put fried rice in my engine
& the Rooster crows, too
red inside spicy ribcage.

The tide of my lungs goes out again
& it is never enough.
Dry rushes back
flooding me with cracked skins of
5,000 onions peeling.
Our cries sauté the winter air &

caramelize the ceiling. She says:
"I can cook this down for you."

The bulbs grow hot in Rooster's mouth
feet beating out spurred indignance:
"Are you awake yet?
Are you awake yet?"
This time
hot words aren't indignant enough to keep me.
And my control knows it's time to climb out
& freeze my fingers down the fractured hillside tilt.

Crisp, just cusped over-mountain sun
burns cold my cracked
onion fingers, as my engine
slowly turns over. On my ride
cut onion thoughts of her,
draw brine to my eyes

& this is what it is to leave her.
She is heat & tail feathers
& ginger simmering away
fried rice that stings the lips alive
& dances fire
deep in all four chambers of my engine.

When we fucked

I watched her use her elbows as a metronome.

Boundaries

This is the poem my hands
are afraid to write
this poem
might break. Her

laughter is beach glass soft,
special freckle in belly
of shoreline,
almost stone her smooth
is a worked-
over mix:
heat, pressure, &
the patience of cooling.

If my tidal arms thrown
wide by moon,
catastrophed past our lovely
grain by grain
exchange & I touched too much—

see,
this is the crash my waves are afraid to make,
the poem of my breaking into her,
changing the shape of her.

Fall after fall
I pull tight her
particles, touch past mineral, hunger
for more than just this slow devouring.

If I touch her there,
on those parts she calls
her "man parts"

gasp
rusting flecks scrape
cataclysm up esophagus
& shatter our common jaw.

Our kinship extinguished.
And dead fish the beached
echo of our genders.

For those seeking my body as passage,

I am sorry.
I am not a proper vessel,
I sometimes allow the swells to toss me
to & fro
just to let my barnacles breathe.

I'm sorry
but I do not turn
when you twist your engines into me.
I am sorry
that the smoke you planted,
hot & coalful in my belly
is now a rising stink
emptied of results intended.

I am sorry,
but your cargo doesn't fit,
& we are taking a detour,
so I can deepen my bonds with the whales
& sirens.

I am sorry
but I will not tell them to soften
their voices.

That uncontrol you think you are feeling,
that "magic" they sang into your skin,
will not justify even one unhinged clasp.

Some might say it's your own fault,
that your ears were just,
unprepared
for their moonsong,
but not me.

I know
all about your innocence.
How the shift from silence to siren can feel
so sudden, so small.

I feel your fear.
And I am sorry
(but) the whales will devour you
& your raw untightened eardrums.

I am sorry I put the force
of you in danger
but this is what you face
when you board me
with your brawn all hung
out & blazing.

See Something? Say Something.

I see senior after senior pulled
aside, each apologizes
for not removing from
bags packed with care & wrinkled
fingers items certain
to be incendiary:
deodorant,
lotion,
a bottle of water she'd meant to
drink while waiting.

I think of my own grandparents.
I shudder,
noticeable to those who stand
directly behind. They look me
over with the disdain that's become
the comfort of the modern traveler.

I see anxieties bristle into
xenophobic bitterness. I see
my thoughts curdle at the sound
of their French, at the sound of Chinese,
& for a moment
it begins
to work. I despise them

for their difference.
I see fears impatient.
I see massed ritual submission.
I see the blind
the resigned.
A gangly teenager raises
her arms for the machine,
smiles big,
shows how much she's bracing.

I see my own resentment
tensing my body,
tensing my face.
I teeter,
sweat tears slow & terse away from skin.

I see them step into the backscatter machine.
More than half are herded
between its black box theatres.
Most assent easily
to its effects untested.

I unbuckle danger from my body
& place all traces of agency
into plastic bins.

I see that it is my turn.
I see the precipice between
metal detector & backscattered invasion.
I see the waiting.
I see the shabby uniform
before he notices me.
I, for a moment, hope,
Maybe he won't.

He sees my naked
feet first. I see his left arm wave me
toward the invasion
machine.
And quiet like a child under
discipline, I use my voice to see
my feelings & say,
"I'm not doing that."

I see his eyes exasperate.
My teeth see the fear
in my lip & push it
back in. I see myself holding up
the line. With fear-flushed pupils
cinching smaller, I see my refusal
as the problem it is causing.

"I see," says the uniform.

And after a wait
provides me with an agent of
my gender as security sees it.

I see the X where she
tells me to stand.
I see her mime the twisted
ritual her brown hands calmly
script the forced intimacy

back of the hand across
the buttocks, twice inside
of the thigh.
"Raise your arms,
face palms to the sky."

I see
the hands now gloved hover
under armpits,
blue behind my shoulders
where their hovering becomes
the seeing I do with my skin.
Muffled under preemptive leggings
the pressure is slow
intentional
more than seeing.

Curb Appeal

It's construction season on the Hill again.
The skyscraping orange
cranes are once again overgrazing.
Coaxed up from the pitted
wounds, luxury rises high.

Slowly crawling up & up.
A monolith of rent hikes &
classist mustaches.
Everything gutted except the quaint facade.

Each time a building goes down
I see a Chase Bank popping up.
Filtered through chain-link veil
the branding clatters in the voice of

bamboo floors that stretch fast & tall.
Sprouting condos,
classy marketing strategies,
hygienic suits,
custom messenger bags,
$80 razor cuts,
& a steady uptick in calls to social services,
concerned citizens requesting a mental health restoration.

Clean young people plastered laughing
on windows
on sidewalks eating
street food with their pristine
teeth, tearing up the grease,
& throwing a block party
for folks who can still afford the neighborhood.

Breaking Up

To My Dearest Seattle,

I love you, but you have broken my heart.

Not swiftly or intentionally, I think, but for three years there's been a crack growing in my chest. This crack's been pulling slowly open from the repetitive tension of lacking that, for so long, went beneath my notice.

I've made love to the grooves of your geography. Found comfort in the crooked of your disagreeing streets. The curling friendship of your neighborhoods has cushioned the empty of my resources these three years we have shared together.

I came to you, Seattle, with my ass freshly kicked out of a rigorous and a sadly less-than-radical teaching program. I showed up with $800 in my pocket and no job guaranteed. I came seeking rebirth, looking to put some roots down. With you I wanted to fuck around, unfurl in ways I was afraid to do while I was digging myself into the debt of college. I let the story of starting fresh seduce me. I believed I could prosper here.

When I arrived I sunk the last of my borrowed money

into you. Dear city, I've spent the time since waiting for a return on that wistful investment. In the three years we've been together I've been out of work more than I've been in it. I worked as a pizza delivery guy and a data entry clerk. I pulled shots at a doomed co-op in the south end. For six weeks I drove through winter's hardest hours in a van full of fresh bread I couldn't afford to buy.

I took a job on a boat giving tours. I proudly told strangers all about your most beautiful features and quietly downed 4 Advil whenever my windowless lunch break rolled around. In some ways I loved it (minus the 10-hour days). Talking about you always brought a smile to my face and almost made those grueling duties worth it. I used to dream about mentioning you and my love for you on the back of my very first bestseller. But your lack of reciprocity has stopped me from dreaming about such things.

I loved you before all of this, before I even came close. Seattle, I loved you before I sunk my trust into your salty soil. It would take me days to list everything I love about you. Every third poem I write is about your body. None of my other lovers can boast this number. But you've never belonged to me. Your salt, whose flavor I love, has continually rejected all of the roots

I've tried to stick into it.

I've moved seven times in the past three years. Your arms may have been open but not always comfortable. Even in this last year, while I've had enough resources to render my poverty invisible, while my address finally stayed the same for a little ... I could feel you shifting, still feel you constricting.

This is tough for me to say. Because if anyone asks me where I am from I will say "Puget Sound born and raised." I'm proud of how constant you've been in my life. I love your fractional politics and your highly visible friction between urban and rural communities. In so many ways we are family, you and I.

I don't even know how to contemplate living someplace without salt in the air. Your breath is all that I know.

But I've begun to prepare my lungs anyway. Started slowly packing a few bags. I'm tired of being the only one of my friends who doesn't pay their own rent.

My dearest Seattle, I simply have no idea how to make it with you. I've always felt at least one step behind your gorgeously rapid cultural beat. I have been intimidated by your purportedly artsy and encouraging communities. Those I've attempted to dip into have always seemed a little too cool for me. And I've been dipping into your icy for long enough to see that it's not just my impostor syndrome anymore. As cultured as you are, Seattle, you are the wrong city for beginners like me.

I am not a prodigy (I gave up this version of myself long ago). I'm actually a lot slower than you think I am. Addicted to the uncertainty of learning, I don't know if you can wait for me to catch up anymore. And as much as I love the way my legs long to race when I see you looking at me, this time I need to resist the way you tug at my sensibilities.

I'm not sure of what I am going to do with this life. With you, Seattle, there is so little room for confusion. I always feel you begging me for a definitive answer to questions my body is not ready to set free. Can't you see? I want to stay in the swill of my curiosity.

Curiosity is my salt.

My health has declined in the last several months. Slower has become a necessity rather than a wise choice. I've been forced to face the pace my body demands. And consequently I've become less able to keep the same commitments I've had in the past. And, my dear city, you've not been any sort of accommodating. I can no longer lead you on like this.

I've never lived anyplace else. So maybe your problems are problems everywhere, for every city. But I'm willing to strike out and see if there's a city out there that might just be a little better for beginners like me.

Seattle, I want to be with you, but you ask so much from me and you don't give back enough for me to stay healthy and honest to the person I aspire to be. So I've decided to leave.

I'm leaving with less money, less hope, and less health than I came to you with. I am leaving to see if I can find or create that which you could not give me.

I'm leaving soon. I might come back in three months, or six, or a year. I know you hate when plans aren't concrete, I do too, but I can't say for sure when I'll be back.

Because I might not come back.

And yes, Seattle, it's true that there are parts of you

I can never leave. I've embedded my identity in your most precious residents, sunk my love poems into your salty pockets, mixed my saliva with the sweat of your distant ocean neck. My bike and I have sliced through your avenues churning, yearning, and howling out '80s power ballads.

Oh the glorious moments we shared! Like the first morning of this year, when I was wildly hungover, you convinced me to climb out to you. You snagged my vision on your distance, on the crisp of your wide cyan embrace. The cold comfort of a mountain range steady behind each of my shoulders pushed me and my bicycle forward. In that open moment, emptied of breath, it was easy to love the pressure of you and to forget how you constrict me, my gorgeous winding saltwater lover.

I love you so much. And I'll send you so many postcards. Thank you for giving me what you did. I think we both wish that it had been enough.

<3
WRM

To B, Sleeping

Tonight you, my lover, are finally sleeping.
December wreaks havoc on all things circadian.
In such limb-slung slumber your bedded body
       swallows its rhythm.

I can hear you calling out dreamy-mouthed
lips sticking, parting:
"Refuge."
Breath quickens
with the blanket slipping.

We spend our winters trading insomnia & adventure.
Tonight I am watching you, my lover, slumber.

I look up
& find the tongue of morning already whet.
The highways cradle early
workers to more productive dreams.
School buses are making their pick-ups,
the city belongs to birds & dump trucks.

Machine Dreams

The sight of you cranks into
my lungs like pistons.
Sharp with this thought,
I find the spots
on your body
where you're tearing open
a new kind of paradox.

You ungender my engine,
fill its chambers with the simple of
numbers,
variables,
reckless algorithms.
Functions collect behind
my neck.
Throat full of possible
outcomes.

Cautiously, I lean my transmission
into you. Gears grind
& quick I twist away from your skin.
You leave
my parts thirsty for grease
& the buzz of churning.

Last night I dreamt my body was a
reciprocal saw. I chewed up
the fuel of your yummy
cedar angles & awoke with a mouthful of dry
sawdust.

Delicious

pieces of the afternoon
steeping pungent in the sweet & beany air,
drunk puns steam up the windows,
high shelved "I" sounds curl to the ceiling,
youth,
we are unafraid of talking about ourselves.

There can be no reverse of the things which tran-
spire in this kitchen.
June 23rd is every bit as full as it could be.
The roundabout calls to every neighborhoodlum,
"Come wait in the sunlight."

A dancing heart is only contained by its chambers.
Four platforms of potential value
a jury of muscled pumppumppumppump.

Wet green bottoms of feet
find earth through grass grown long all spring.
Lush yellow roses outweigh their ambitions,
droop even under tongue of mother sun.

Bowls of varying sizes
cupped in six hands,
thirty fingers working toward the same destination
& it is delicious.

Wander–Ponder

First dusk on Spencer Spit,
as sun dipped brief
between cloud cover & mountain,
a rainbow erupted. Its
full spectrum spine arched
across eastern sky.
Purple roots sprang up
from the cleave of two unnamed islands.
The colors buried their ending
deep in a grove of Frost Island pines.

Beneath this dusky low-slung sunset
my companion
hushes out

long low sentences,
"I would bet,
that this wetland replenishes the entire area's water
table."

I smile,
let "replenish" splash against my eardrums.
Later
& completely by accident
he rhymes the words

"wander" &
"ponder."

We talk
about our newfound distance,
"How far we've come
from the urban demand
to document & divulge."

"This distance will force us to experience
experiences."

His eyes fix on my violet blossom notebook.
The fire pit opens its cedar throat
crackles,
"Writing this poem is different from recording.

A poem is not a record."
A poem is an artifact
a plaster cast of a cloven hoof
a fish stuck in the nourishing decay of a riverbed.
Poetry is always in motion.

For dinner we shared fish with the eagles,
congratulating each other on accomplishments
culinary & athletic.

Four wheels between us
& 72 spokes each,
thousands of leg extensions
push soleus motions up through kneecap to quadricep.

Our bodies build muscular algorithms
as paths extend at our backs.

Our muscles are not records.
Records are dead
motionless things.
Our muscles are alive.

Bridge by Bridge

Olympic mountains, capped wet white,
slick tight like latex melting.
Crocus buds cluster
& shadow flies mossy
across culvert.

Legs like wings
in open sprocket
thighs churn wild.

Sweat gathers
in the switchbacks pooling.
Hungry.
I take them on,
bridge by bridge,
lungs pumping spring into spring.

Sibling Rivalry

We Crackerjack boxed
under the slats of picnic pine
exchanged slingshot thoughts
landing insult after insult.
Among the jostling khaki thighs we whispered,
"Piss face," "Hairy toe," "Spaz."

Spitseed watermelon
war mouths slicked
antagonistic & sticky
with the love of sibling rivalry,

I loved you with fist
& shinbones kicking,
how when the gendered tools
tried to dictate our play
we shoved Polly into the Pocket
of a Hot Wheels truck bed.

We slapjacked till backs of hands
flushed red as the hearts
our elders played for petty cash & bragging rights.

I know we didn't always get along.
I know I one time put pepper

in your swimming trunks,
but there's really no other way I can remember us being.

Even when we used our bodies in the game of conflict
we were still
somehow getting along.

Road Trip

The dashboard overflowed with numbers and we wetted our hands in paling green pickle juice. Jumped naked into a cold ocean. Came out with mouthfuls of kelp and salt. We stopped for sandwiches and peed in a field. The fennel cracked and breathed a licorice dust in the hot yellow afternoon. Even the shadows collected some gold flecks that were more than just dust, I'm sure.

We stopped for every hitchhiker. Even let some of them fuck in the back of our humming bread truck as we fried eggs in the sand. Low slung propane between the dunes we made a mess of the pancake batter. We gave whiskey to street performers because we did not have any quarters left. Spent $10 a day until our pockets ran dry.

On the first hooked leg of the trip the forest nearly ate us. Highway 1 breathed purple down our necks, slipped us into danger with switchbacking slings and swallows.

Two thin-necked mandolins made small talk and between all of that we picked up Thea. She drew a pirate on our naked pine siding. "I've been doing this since I was fifteen." She told the best jokes, dirty and otherwise, fetched us food still-warm from the prizingest of dumpsters. Girl knew all of the tricks, lived large, and made grand, exceptional laughter. Allergic to sleeping under city skies, she was all love and endearments. Lit her cigarettes like they were candles for the hopeless.

In those licorice fields we didn't know who owned what part of the land. How overgrown the "No Trespassing" signs had become. We sang a few songs and watched the highway float above us. We saw elk, like icebergs, in the tall grasses. Only visible from the eyes up. I still haven't looked at the photographs.

I ate a hamburger for the first time in two years and slept all the way back to the ocean. We squirmed under arching freeway limbs. Sometimes those endless concrete arms collided so violently, we were locked in the interstate sway of two gargantuan cephalopods screwing.

All the way down we lived on tuna fish sandwiches. The road called out our names with repeating yellow tongues and I hope she calls me back one day. Her cracked asphalt voice is one I have begun to silence with empty pocket excuses and a sad sack of somedays.

And I miss her. In conjunction with the whirring roundness of rubber and the old engine reluctantly turning over, I miss her voice the most.

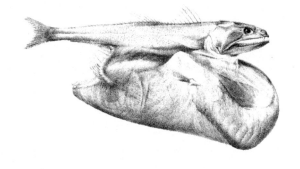

Publication Notes

"Elle" was published in *Skin to Skin*

"Babydoll & Spatula" was published in *Wilde Magazine*

"Primer for the Docent" was published in *Cactus Heart*

Acknowledgments

This book would not have been possible without the coaching of Tara Hardy, the instructors at the Bent Writing Institute, and the slew of fantastic writing teachers I've had the great fortune to learn from: Sandy Yannone, Kate Crow, Cody Pherigo, Kay Powers, and my fifth grade teacher Ms. Phillips.

I'd also like to thank my deeply gracious and patient editor Amy Chadwick. Her attention and generosity proved invaluable when it came to whipping these poems into shape.

Big thanks go out to the city of Seattle and the four gorgeous bikes that helped me reveal some of its secrets. (RIP McFly. You were adequately scrappy.)

I'm so grateful for the gorgeous and risky writing that I've had the luck to dip my heart into. Without the works of Audre Lorde, Andrea Gibson, Rainer Maria Rilke, Kim Addonizio, Lawrence Ferlinghetti, Roald Dahl, and many many more, my life and my writing practices would be impossible.

Extra special thanks go out to my generous and tender life partner Strand whose unwavering belief in my writing, my capacity for love, and my squishy little gender means more than I will ever be able to express.

About the Author

Wryly T. McCutchen is a ferociously genderqueer poet, blogger, and all around trouble maker. They love bikes and anything else with simple exposed mechanics. In 2013 Wryly was listed as a finalist in Write Bloody Publishing's competition and has had their poetry and nonfiction appear in *Wilde Magazine, Alive With Vigor,* and *Raven Chronicles.* Wryly currently runs a personal/political blog called *Meet Me in the Margins* and holds an MFA in creative nonfiction and poetry from Antioch University.

┌─ **THIS BOOK IS ONE OF THE MANY AVAILABLE FROM** ─┐

HƎLL PЯƎSS
UNIVERSITY OF HELL PRESS

└──────── **DO YOU HAVE THEM ALL?** ────────┘

by TYLER ATWOOD
an electric sheep jumps to greener pasture

by JOHN W BARRIOS
Here Comes the New Joy

by EIREAN BRADLEY
the I in team
the little BIG book of go kill yourself

by SUZANNE BURNS
Boys

by CALVERO
someday i'm going to marry Katy Perry
i want love so great it makes Nicholas Sparks cream
in his pants

by MICHAEL MCLAUGHLIN
Countless Cinemas

by JOHNNY NO BUENO
We Were Warriors

by A.M. O'MALLEY
Expecting Something Else

by STEPHEN M. PARK
High & Dry
The Grass Is Greener

by CHRISTINE RICE
Swarm Theory

by MICHAEL N. THOMPSON
A Murder of Crows

by SARAH XERTA
Nothing to Do with Me

edited by CAM AWKWARD-RICH & SAM SAX
The Dead Animal Handbook: An Anthology of
Contemporary Poetry

CPSIA information can be obtained
at www.ICGtesting.com
Printed in the USA
LVOW03s0741180218
566966LV00005B/99/P